Legendary Mermaids

COLORING BOOK

MARTY NOBLE

DOVER PUBLICATIONS
GARDEN CITY, NEW YORK

Explore under the sea with 31 stunning scenes featuring beautiful mermaids and mermen from countries on six continents as well as islands around the world. From millennia-old mythological figures such as Thessalonike (Greece) and Atargatis (Syria) to recent popular culture icons like "The Little Mermaid" (Denmark) and Dyesebel (the Philippines), each exquisitely detailed drawing invites you to add your own colorful touches. Captions identifying the name of the mermaid or story depicted—as well as the country, region, or tribe of origin—can be found on each page, to the left of the perforation line. The images are printed on one side only, and the pages are perforated for easy removal and display of your finished artwork.

Bibliographical Note

Legendary Mermaids Coloring Book is a new work, first published by Dover Publications in 2021. Thirty of the illustrations originally appeared in *Mythical Mermaids Coloring Book*, published by Dover in 2012, and sixteen of those illustrations have been revised. One new illustration has been added.

International Standard Book Number

ISBN-13: 978-0-486-84849-5
ISBN-10: 0-486-84849-3

Manufactured in the United States of America
84849301
www.doverpublications.com

2 4 6 8 10 9 7 5 3 1

2021